Tundra 16

BE A BEE 19

COLOURS AND SMELLS

Woodlands 20

MYSTERY SEEDS 23

FRUITS AND SEEDS

Water plants 24

MAKE A POND 27

NEW PLANTS FROM OLD

OXYGEN IN WATER

More things to learn about plants 28

BE A WILD FLOWER SPOTTER 29

Glossary 30

Index 32

Words in **bold** are explained in the Glossary on pages 30-31.

All kinds of plants

Trees, the grass you play on and water lilies floating on ponds and lakes are all plants. Look for plants growing everywhere – in the soil, in water and even on walls.

carpel

petal

stamens

Poppies

Aubretia

Pansies

PICTURE SEARCH
★ search for flowers of different colours, shapes and sizes
★ search for leaves of different shapes and sizes

Ground elder

Cornflowers

Miniature conifers

Dandelions

Bindweed

Start Science

Plants

Sally Hewitt

Chrysalis Children's Books

First published in the UK in 2003 by
Chrysalis Children's Books
An imprint of Chrysalis Books Group Plc
The Chrysalis Building, Bramley Road,
London W10 6SP

Paperback edition first published in 2005

ISBN 1 84138 271 X (hb)
ISBN 1 84458 299 X (pb)

British Library Cataloguing in Publication Data
for this book is available from the British Library.

Editorial Manager: Joyce Bentley
Senior Editor: Sarah Nunn
Editorial Assistant: Clare Chambers
Project Editor: Jean Coppendale
Designers: Rachel Hamdi and Holly Mann
Illustrators: Joanna Partis, Sara Walker
and Gwyneth Williamson
Educational consultants: Sally Morgan
and Helen Walters

Printed in China

Contents

All kinds of plants 4

DISCOVER THE PARTS OF A PLANT 7

GROW BEANS

Desert plants 8

HOW DO PLANTS DRINK? 11

ESCAPING WATER

HEADS UP

Rainforests 12

SUN-LOVING PLANTS 15

MAKE A GREENHOUSE

Sweet pea

Ivy

Moss

Wall flowers

Candy tuft

Buttercups

Marsh marigolds

Lilac allium

Water lilies

Lupins

Pink allium

Alyssum

Rock jasmine

Atlas daisies

5

How plants grow

Trees are the biggest plants of all. They have thick, woody **trunks** to hold them up as they grow towards the light.

Plants with flowers

Many plants have flowers. Flowers can be big or small and come in all different colours.

Plants with no flowers

Moss is a kind of plant with no flowers. New moss grows from spores, which look like tiny specks of dust.

Life cycle of a flowering plant

A sweet pea produces many seeds before it dies, which grow into new sweet pea plants.

1 A bee visits the flower to drink sweet juice called **nectar**.

2 Yellow dust called pollen brushes on to the bee. The bee carries the pollen to another flower.

4 New sweet pea plants grow from the seeds.

3 The flower uses the pollen to make seeds, which fall to the ground.

DISCOVER THE PARTS OF A PLANT

If you buy a young plant, take a look before you plant it in the garden or window box. Or pull up a weed such as a dandelion. Spread the plant out on white paper so you can see the roots, stem, leaves and flowers.

Flower

The flower is the part of the plant where seeds are made

Stem

The stem supports the plant and takes water to the flower and leaves

Leaves

Plants use sunlight to make food in green leaves

Roots

Tiny hairs on the roots take up water

 WARNING: Ask an adult to help you with all the activities in this book.

GROW BEANS

A bean is a seed. Inside a bean is a new tiny plant.

Soak some broad beans from a seed packet in water. Line a jam jar with damp kitchen towels then push about 3 beans between the towels and the glass.

Watch the beans grow a root and a shoot. Plant a new bean plant in some soil and give it all it needs to grow – air, water and light.

Desert plants

Plants have found ways to grow in deserts where it can be baking hot in the day, freezing cold at night and where very little rain falls.

Saguaro cactus

Ocotillo

Pincush cactus

spine clusters

flowers

Beaver tail cactus

Barrel cactus

Organ
pipe
cactus

hairline
spines

Prickly pear
cactus

...ollen
...m

Desert peonies

PICTURE SEARCH
★ search for plants with **spines**
★ search for plants that store
water in their swollen stems

9

Growing with very little water

Seeds lie in the desert sand until a rain storm brings them to life in a burst of colour.

Waxy leaves and stems

The leaves and stems of many desert plants are covered in a thick, waxy layer to stop water escaping.

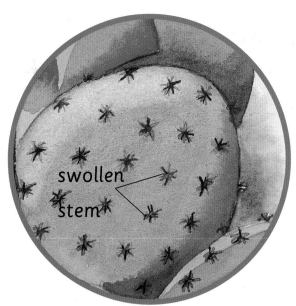

swollen stem

Storing water

The beaver tail cactus stores water in its swollen stem. It is covered in small spines that are like hairs.

Spine clusters

The spines of the barrel cactus grow in groups or clusters. Animals have to be careful when they pick its juicy fruit.

spine clusters

✏ HOW DO PLANTS DRINK?

Plants draw water up from the ground through little hairs on their roots. The water goes up the stem and into every part of the plant. Some water then evaporates into the air through the leaves.

celery stem

coloured water

Add some food colouring to a glass of water. Now put a stick of celery into the coloured water.

You will *see* the coloured water rising up the tubes inside the celery stem.

✏ ESCAPING WATER

Water escapes from plants into the air through tiny holes in their leaves.

Cover a house plant with a clear plastic bag. After a while, you will *see* drops of water on the sides of the bag.

plastic bag

See what happens if you try this with a cactus or a plant with waxy leaves.

✏ HEADS UP

Pick a dandelion, buttercup or any other flowering weed with a green stem. Put in a jar without water and watch it droop.

Now add water and see it stand up and raise its flower head.

Rainforests

It is dark, hot and wet in the rainforest.
Plants grow high in the branches of the tall
rainforest trees where they can reach the sunlight.

toucan

Lianas

macaw

Arum
lily

tapir

tarantula

Stinkhorn
fungus

spider monkey

Orchids

Bromeliad

jaguar

humming bird

anana tree

PICTURE SEARCH
★ search for **lianas** growing around tree trunks
★ search for plants growing on branches

Hibiscus

Epiphytes

leaf cutter ants

Ginger plant

poison arrow frog

viper

13

Reaching for light

A **canopy** of huge leaves high above the ground keeps out the rain and sun so rainforest plants find different ways to search for light and water.

Lianas

Lianas or vines are climbing plants. They wrap themselves around tree trunks and branches and climb up to reach the light.

Lianas or vines

Living on air

Plants called epiphytes grow on trees where their leaves can trap sunlight and their roots **absorb** water from the damp air.

Epiphytes

Swimming pool

Bromeliad flowers collect rainwater in their petals and make a swimming pool for water animals.

Bromeliad

SUN-LOVING PLANTS

Plants need sunlight to grow because they use **energy** from the sun to make food in their green leaves.

Cut out shapes from card. Using re-usable adhesive, stick the shapes onto the leaves of a house plant. Put the plant in sunlight.

After about two weeks, take the shapes off the leaves. Underneath, you will see a yellow shape where the sunlight couldn't shine on the green leaf.

MAKE A GREENHOUSE

Sprinkle some grass seeds on soil in a seed tray. Put the tray in a sunny place outside and water it. Cut a plastic bottle in half and cover some of the seeds. The sun heats the air inside the bottle.

Watch how the seeds grow faster in the warmer air under the bottle.

15

Tundra

No tall trees grow in the tundra because of the strong winds and ice and snow cover the ground all winter. Many animals arrive to feed on the plants that flower in the short summer.

Birch

Canada geese

Bilberry

Arctic hares

Alpine sorrel

Arctic poppies

Reindeer moss

Arctic terns

reindeer

Purple saxifrage

Spruce

Dwarf willow

Bewick's swans

Wild rosemary

PICTURE SEARCH
★ search for short bushes and trees
★ search for plants growing low over the ground

Short bushes

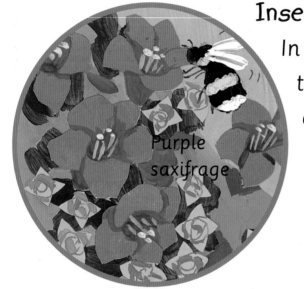

Bushes in the tundra are short and have small leaves. This helps to protect them from the fierce, icy winds.

Insects and flowers

In the tundra, swarms of insects feed on the colourful, scented flowers. They carry pollen from flower to flower.

Purple saxifrage

Arctic poppies

Insects drink sweet nectar from the flowers. This gives the insects energy to survive the cold weather.

Reindeer moss

In the tundra, reindeer moss covers a lot of the ground and makes good food for hungry herds of reindeer all year round.

 ## BE A BEE!

The pollen of some flowers sticks onto the back of a visiting bee and sometimes to its head or legs as well.

Wrap some tape – sticky side out – around the end of your finger and pretend it's a bee. Gently push the 'bee' into the middle of a flower then pull it out. Use a magnifying glass to see where the pollen has stuck to the tape.

 ## COLOURS AND SMELLS

Flowers are brightly coloured and smell sweet to attract insects.

Tie together the stems of some sweet scented flowers such as roses. Hang them upside down in a warm, dry place.

When the petals have dried out, shake off the petals and put them in a bowl. They will make a sweet smelling **pot-pourri**.

Woodlands

In woodlands, some trees have leaves like needles and some have shiny green leaves. In autumn, many trees lose their leaves. All woodland trees and plants produce different kinds of seeds.

Rowan tree

Maple leaves

Red oak tree

Maple seed

seeds

wings

Rosehips

Blackberries

Burdock

Conker

seed case

Pine tree

Beech tree

Sweet chestnut tree

PICTURE SEARCH
★ search for berries and brown nuts
★ search for trees that lose their leaves

squirrel

Holly berries

kers

Thistle flower

Acorn

Thistle

Spreading seeds

Plants spread their seeds in all kinds of ways. Animals help to spread seeds by eating, carrying and storing nuts and berries.

Food stores

Squirrels forget where they bury their winter stores of nuts, and some nuts then grow into trees.

Droppings

Birds eat juicy berries. The seeds inside the berries fall to the ground in the bird's droppings.

Hooks

Burdock seeds cling onto animal fur with tiny hooks and are carried to a new place to grow.

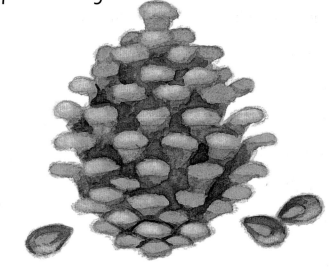

Pine cones

When pine cones open up you can see the seeds inside them.

MYSTERY SEEDS

Find out which *seeds* have landed in a patch of earth.

In early spring, collect soil from three different places . Put the earth in three different seed trays and label them.

Water the earth in the trays and you may be surprised to discover what grows after a few weeks.

FRUITS AND SEEDS

Fruit is the part of a plant that contains the *seeds*.

Collect some fruit such as an apple, a banana, a melon, a tomato and some pea **pods**. Ask an adult to help you cut them open and look for the seeds inside. You could try planting the seeds. They might grow into a new plant.

23

Water plants

When you go to a pond or stream, look out for tall plants growing on the banks, plants floating on the surface and plants swaying underwater.

Yellow irises

dragonfly

Reeds

Water lily

Greater spearwort

Canadian pondweed

Hornwort

seeds

Brown reed mace

mayfly

PICTURE SEARCH
★ search for leaves that float on the top of the water
★ search for tall pointed leaves on the banks

Marsh marigolds

frog

ater boatmen

Duckweed

pond skaters

Canadian pondweed

pond snail

Fanwort

water beetle

Growing by the water

Underwater plants that grow in ponds and streams have long stems and feathery leaves. They move in the flowing water.

Leaf boats

Water lily leaves are flat and shiny. They float like little boats on the pond and make a resting place for small animals.

flower

Water lily

lily pad

seeds

Brown reedmace

Seed heads

Brown reedmace grow on the banks of ponds. Their heads are packed with seeds that fly away on the wind.

Canadian pondweed

Canadian pondweed grows very quickly. It makes a good hiding place for small water animals. Water snails lay their eggs on its leaves.

Canadian pondweed

MAKE A POND

Spread some gravel over the bottom of an old washing up bowl. Add a little soil and a large stone. Carefully pour in some rainwater. Buy some pondweed and plant it by holding it down underwater with stones.

Watch out for water animals visiting your pond.

NEW PLANTS FROM OLD

Break off a small piece of Canadian pondweed and put it in a bowl of rainwater. It will quickly grow into a new plant.

OXYGEN IN WATER

Water plants fill the water with bubbles of oxygen as they make food using sunlight.

Add a few strands of pond weed in a clear jar. Put the jar in a warm sunny place. Look carefully, and after a while you will see tiny bubbles in the water.

27

More things to learn about plants

What kind of tree?

You can tell whether a tree is an evergreen or a deciduous tree by looking at its leaves.

Evergreens

Evergreen trees keep their leaves all year round. Some leaves are tough and shiny to protect them in all kinds of weather.

Conifers

Conifers are a type of evergreen tree. They have long thin leaves called needles that can stay on the trees throughout very cold winters.

Deciduous trees

Deciduous trees have big, green leaves. Before winter, the leaves change colour and die, and fall to the ground. New leaves grow again in the spring.

Flower shapes

Look out for flowers with these different shapes:

All in one

A daisy and a sunflower are really lots of flowers all in one flower head. Each petal and yellow 'disc' are little flowers called florets.

Bells

Some flowers are shaped like a bell. Insects have to crawl right inside them to drink the nectar.

Circles

Can you see how this flower is made up of a pattern of circles? The petals form a circle around the centre.

HOW TO BE A WILD FLOWER SPOTTER

★ Use your eyes. Some wild flowers are very small. Sometimes they hide very close to the ground, under big leaves or among tall grasses.

★ Note down where a wild flower is growing and the date you spotted it.

★ Use all your senses. You might smell a flower before you see it, or hear the buzzing of visiting insects.

You need:

★ a magnifying glass to look closely at the flower

★ a notebook and coloured pencils to copy the shape and colour of the flower and leaves

★ a pocket wild flower guide to help you find out the name of the flowers you spot

Be careful

★ look where you are treading. Try not to step on wild flowers.

★ never pick or pull up wild flowers. Leave them for other people to enjoy.

29

Glossary

Absorb

Absorb means to take in. Tiny hairs on the roots of plants absorb water from the soil or from the air.

Banks

The sides of a river or a stream are called banks. Plants grow on riverbanks in the wet, muddy soil.

Cacti

Cacti are plants that have found ways to grow in hot, dry deserts. They have thick stems for storing water and spines to protect them from hungry and thirsty animals.

Canopy

The canopy is where the leaves of tall rainforest trees and other plants form a roof high above the ground, keeping out most of the sunlight.

Energy

Plants need energy to grow. They use energy from the sun to make food in their green leaves.

Nectar

Flowering plants make a sweet juice called nectar in the centre of their flowers to attract insects and birds.

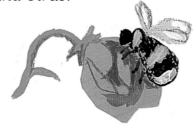

Oxygen

Oxygen is a gas found in the air and in water. We take in oxygen when we breathe and plants help give out oxygen through their leaves.

Pods

Many plants have a fruit called a pod to hold their seeds. You can split open a pea pod and find juicy green peas inside that are good to eat. Peas are seeds of the pea plant.

Pollen

Pollen is the yellow dust flowers need to make new seeds. A flower can only make new seeds when pollen is carried from one flower to another.

Pot-pourri

A pot-pourri is a mixture of petals that give out a sweet smell. It can be used to fill a room with a beautiful scent of flowers.

Spines

Spine is another word for prickle. Cactus plants have spines instead of leaves to stop precious water escaping. Prickly spines also make cacti painful to eat.

Spores

Mushrooms, toadstools, ferns and mosses all give out spores instead of seeds. Like seeds, spores will become new plants if they land in a good place to grow.

Surface

The surface of something means its top covering. A water lily leaf for example floats on the surface of a pond or lake.

Trunks

A tree trunk is a very thick, woody stem. A trunk needs to be strong enough to hold up the tree.

Tundra

Tundra is the name for the land near the Arctic where no tall trees grow and the summers are very short. Just below the surface, the soil is frozen all year round.

Vines

Vines are plants with long stems that climb walls and curl around other plants. A liana is a kind of vine that grows in rainforests.

Wax

Some plants have a waxy covering on their leaves, which makes them shiny and waterproof.

Weeds

A weed is the name for a wild plant that gardeners and farmers haven't chosen to put in their gardens or fields. They usually get rid of weeds so their crops can grow.

Index

animals 12-13, 16-17, 22

banks 30
beans: growing 7
bees 6, 19
berries 22
bird droppings 22
bromeliads 13, 14
bushes: short 18

cacti 8-9, 10, 30
canopy 14, 30
conifers 28

deciduous trees 28
deserts 8-11
duckweed 26

energy 15, 30
epiphytes 13, 14
evergreens 28

flowers 4-5, 6, 7
   colours 19
   shapes 28
   smell 19
   wild flowers 29
fruit 23

grass 4
greenhouse: making 15

hooked seeds 22

insects 18

leaves 4, 7
   floating 24-5
   of trees 20
   waxy 9, 10
lianas 12, 14
life cycle 6
light 14-15

moss 6, 16

nectar 6, 30
nuts 22

oxygen 27, 30

pine cones 22
plants:
   how they grow 6-7
   parts 7
   types 4-5
pods 30
pollen 6, 18, 19, 30
pollination 18
pond: making 27
pondweed 27
pot-pourri 19, 31

rainforests 12-15
reindeer moss 16, 18
roots 7

seeds 6, 18, 20, 23
   how they are spread 22
spines 8, 9, 10, 31
spores 6, 31
stems 7, 10
sunlight 15
surface 31

trees 4, 6, 20-1, 28
trunks 6, 31
tundra 16-19, 31

vines 31

water:
   escaping from plant 11
   how plants drink 11
   storage methods 10
water lilies 4, 5, 26
water plants 24-7
wax 10, 31
weeds 11, 31
wild flower spotter 29
woodlands 20-3